100 Days
of
Thanksgiving
Devotional

100 Days
of
Thanksgiving
Devotional

Michael E Zito I

INTRODUCTION

God's Steadfast Love last forever
A Psalm for Giving Him Thankfulness.

(PSALM 100:1-5)
A psalm. For giving grateful praise.
Shout for joy to the Lord, all the earth.
Worship the Lord with gladness;
come before him with joyful songs.
Know that the Lord is God.
It is he who made us, and we are his[a];
we are his people, the
sheep of his pasture.
Enter his gates with thanksgiving
and his courts with praise;
give thanks to him and praise his name.
For the LORD is good and his love
endures forever; his faithfulness
continues through all generations.

DAY ONE AND TWO

- Thank you Father God ABBA
  for your patience with me.

- Thank God for the rain and the snow.

- Thank you LORD for all the
  different verses in the Bibles.

- Thank you for the Dear that come
  through. Hear may they live long
  and Multiply by the hundreds

- May all the wildlife that passes be at
  peace here Thank you for their peace,
  Thank you for the animal's safety.

- Thank you Father for this apple pie.

- Thank you Jesus the Christ
  for being my king

- Thank You Lord for being my savior

- Thank you Holy Spirit for your presence

- Thank you for drawing me into you.

- Thank You father for unfailing LOVE!

Write Something that you're thankful for:

DAY THREE

- Thank you Lord for Christian TV.

- Thank you Father for this cup
  of coffee and this Banana

- Thank you LORD for a safe
  top to town and back

- Father thank for making F3 a Reality

- Father thank you for this
  lemon pie and coffee

- Thank for TV's and remote controls

- Thank you Father for John Hagee Ministers

- Father thank you for having
  preachers share - your wants with
  me. I Love to hear your words

- Thank you my Father God for giving me
  not only the power to get wealth but - the
  millions upon millions of the dollars- to
  prove I have the money to share forth the
  Manifest dollars to prove it!!! hallelujah!!!

- Lord thank you for Brother Allan
  Jackson and His Family and Ministry.

Write Something that you're thankful for:

....

....

....

....

....

....

....

....

....

....

....

....

DAY FOUR

**(1Thessalonians 5:18)
"In everything give thanks; for this is
God's will for you in Christ Jesus."**

- Thank you LORD for waking me
up and getting me out of Bed

- Thank you Father for the wind and the Rain

- Thank you LORD for your
mercies is forever.

- Thank you my LORD for making
Healthier and Healthier

- Thank the Father for teaching
me your words- Help me be a
good teacher of the same.

- Father thank you for Joyce Meyer.
Please keep Her Healthy - and strong

- Father thank you for my healthy
Wife Debbie and her dined table.

- Father thank you for the CD's
und stereo Debbi brought to our
home our camp sight one.

Write Something that you're thankful for:

DAY FIVE

(1 Thessalonians 5:18)
"In everything give thanks; for this is
God's will for you in Christ Jesus."

Thank you Holy Father for the
Fruit of your Holiness!

Which as follows;

- LOVE & Peace, - Kindness, Joy, Patience, Goodness and Faithfulness

- Thank you Father FOR Readiness!

- For your awareness

- Thanks for the Readiness of faith.

- Thank you Father for a safe day.

Write Something that you're thankful for:

DAY SIX

- Thank you Lord for Your strength

- Thank you Lord for coffee
and for the Banns

- Thank You for Dr. Jeremiah and
this ministry family and friend.

- Thank you Father for in
touch with Charlie Stanly

- Father thank you for the Holy
Spirit. Thank you, your strength, I
am week but You are strong.

Write Something that you're thankful for:

DAY SEVEN

- Father thank you for helping me renew my mind.

- Father thank you for giving me another chance to do what's right

- Father thank you for the music

- Father thank you for the medicine

- Father thank you for Health Care

- Father thank you for the money. That you provide

- Father thank you for such a nice day cot.

- Father thank you for taking care of my Love ones

- Father thank you for my wife

- Holy Spirit thank you for helping me do life right

Write Something that you're thankful for:

DAY EIGHT

- Thank You HOLY Spirit for your unfailing guide ness.

- Thank you Holy Angels for Your Faithfulness to serve Father.

- Thank You LORD for the VAN.

- Thank you father for your strength in me.

- Thank you Father for a place to seek you!

- Thank you' Lord for friends and family

- Thank your Father for loving me Thank you for the faith that Believes Your LOVE

- Thank you Father for this Place! hallelujah!

Write Something that you're thankful for:

DAY NINE

- Father, thank you getting me up today.

  - Father thank you for watching
over me in the night.

- Father thank you for taking good care
OF LA DAVE

- Father Thank you for you (who you care)

- Father Thank you for another Banana

- Father thank you for making me awake,
Her for your Glory and fame please!

  - Thank you for Loving me so much

    - Father thank you for helping
me pay the Bills

- Father God thank you for helping me
be renewed, spirit soul, mind, Body

Write Something that you're thankful for:

DAY TEN

- Thank You Father for helping me pays
  - my debt to people and companies.

- Thank you LORD for being so good to me.

- Thank You Father for your great
  WORDS to me and the Church.

- Father thank you for the abundant
  life you have given us.

- Thank You Father for being strong in me.

- Father thank you for making me a
  blessing to the people I move to do.

- Thank You Father for the chair I sit on.

- Father thank you for getting
  me out of bed today

- Father Thank you for a Healthy Pen

- Father Thank you for the rain that is coming

Write Something that you're thankful for:

....

....

....

....

....

....

....

....

....

....

....

....

DAY ELEVEN

- Thank You Father for taking
such a good care of me.

- Thank You Father for all these trees.

- Thank you for making me a blessing

- Thank You Father for getting my hopes up.

- Father Thank You for the
people who help me do life.

- Thank you Holy Spirit for drawing me
closer and closer to being filled and filled and
always kept being filled with you LORD.

- Thank you Farther for your
son setting free from evil

- Father thank you for making me healthy
wealthy and wise been my years

- Father thank you for the Hill song channel

Write Something that you're thankful for:

....

....

....

....

....

....

....

....

....

....

....

....

DAY TWELVE

- Thank You Father for your son Jesus

- Thank You Jess for the Holy Spirit.

- Thank You HOLY Spirit for Counseling

- Thank You Father for HOLY
  Spirit comforting

- Thank You Father for the rain

- Thank You Father for all seasons

- Thank You Father for food and clothing

- Thank You Father for this Home

- Thank You Father for leading me
  in the way you want for me

- Thank You Father for Joy, Peace, strength

- Thank You Father for fire wood

- Thank you Father for my Bed

Write Something that you're thankful for:

DAY THIRTEEN

- Thank You Father for being such a good father.

- Thank You Father for never ever leaving me alone.

- Thank you Father for music.

- Thank you Father for not taking David home yet.

- Father Thank You for saving me from today

- Thank You Father for giving me strength today

Write Something that you're thankful for:

DAY FOURTEEN

- Thanks Father for Ernie and his Zeal.

- Thank You Father for keeping me
safe in you for 63 years today.

- Thank You LORD for a sunny day.

- Thank You Father for a washer and dryer

- Father thank you for taking
care of LA DAVE

- Thank You Father for trusting me.

- Thank You Heavenly Father for
your Faithfulness to me and mind.

- Thank Your Holy spirit for growing me up
with more and more Revelation of everything
that pertains to this life and Godliness

Write Something that you're thankful for:

DAY FIFTEEN

- Thank You Father for tracking mercy.

  - Thank You Father for a gad
    Heath care provider

  - Thank You Father for transportation

- Thank You Father for giving me straight

- Thank You Father God for bearing every
  hurt and every sting of betrayal at the cross.

  - Father, I thank you that Jesus teak
    sickness and poverty at the cross.

Write Something that you're thankful for:

DAY SIXTEEN

(1 Thessalonians 5:18)
"In everything give thanks; for this is
God's will for you in Christ Jesus."

- Thank You Father for your LOVE

(John 3:16)
"For God so loved the world, that
he gave his only begotten Son, that
whosoever believeth in him should not
perish, but have everlasting life."

- Thank you Father for waking
me up to our bed

(Ecclesiastes 3:7)
"a time to tear and a time to mend, a
time to be silent and a time to speak"

- Thank you Father for making me healthy.

- Thank you Father for
counseling me to proper.

- Thank you Father for helping me do what
it is that you would have me to do today.

- Thank you Father for being a faithful God.

- Thank you Father for being
a man that doesn't Lie

(Numbers 23:19)
God is not man, that he should lie, or a
son of man, that he should change his
mind. Has he said, and will he not do it?
Or has he spoken, and will he not fulfill it?

- Thank you Father for being a just God.

- Thank you Father for being a merciful God.

- Thank you Father for being
a Gracious God.

- Thank you Father that you are
a miracle working God.

- Thank you Father for
making me courageous

Write Something that you're thankful for:

DAY SEVENTEEN

- Father for your Faithfulness.

- Thank you Father for hacking
Randy brings me food and drink.

- Thank you Father for the
tomatoes and lettuce.

- Thank You Feather for
another day of Worship.

- Thank You Father for your grace,
grace and more grace, Amen, Amen

- Thank you Father for our home.

- Thank you Feather for daily bread

- Thank you Father for giving us everything
that pertains to life and Godly living

- Thank you father for your daily presence

- Thank you Father that I was
made (born) a woman

Write Something that you're thankful for:

DAY EIGHTEEN

- Thank You Father for letting me know that you are and will always be Faithful to me

- Thank You Father for new clothes and for the Cake (Birthday cake)

- Thank you Father for taking to me

- Thank you Father for the Bibles

- Thank you Father for Bible dictionaries

- Thank you Father for Music

- Thank you Father for Debbie's stereo. (Boom box)

- Thank you Father for the florist and trees.

- Thank you father for the VAN.

- Thank you Father for my motorcycle.

Write Something that you're thankful for:

    MICHAEL E ZITO I

DAY NINETEEN

- Father thank you for
teaching me your LOVE

- Father God thank you for teaching
me how to truly worship you and
what that looks like and feels like.

- Father thank you for the new
clothes shirts and pants.

- Father thank you for that
cake, it tastes good

- Father thank you for getting
me at of bed. Again!

- Father thank you for those Christmas caps.

- Thank you Father my Dad. Thank you for
telling me with Revelation that it is possible
indeed feasible to Pray without ceasing.

(Thessalonians 5:17)
"17 pray without ceasing, 18 give thanks
in all circumstances; for this is the
will of God in Christ Jesus for you."

Write Something that you're thankful for:

DAY TWENTY

- Thank You Father for getting me up!

- Thank You Father for feeding me your word

- Thank you Father for Healing me

- Thank you Father for making me new.

- Father thank you for plating of
  food as well as daily Bread.

Write Something that you're thankful for:

DAY TWENTY - ONE

- Thank you Father God for giving me grace

- Father thank you for making
me right in you.

- Thank you Father for healing my body.

- Thank you Father for healing my mind.

- Thank you Father for sanctifying
me completely and making me whole
spirit, soul, body, at the coming of
(our) my Lord Jesus Christ,

- Thank you Father for keeping me kept

- Father, I thank you that at my lowest
paint, in my darkest hour, the light of
your favor still shines through me

Write Something that you're thankful for:

DAY TWENTY - TWO

- Thank you Father for another beautiful day.

- Thank you Father for giving me a new day.

- Thank you Father for a home and future.

- Thank you Father for giving
  me people to help me.

- Thank you Father for all
  your wonderful creation

- Thank you Father for the Van

- Thank you Father for a saving accounts

- Thank you Father for traveling Grace.

Write Something that you're thankful for:

DAY TWENTY - THREE

• Thank You Father GOD I Love you, you have given me a great day. I am truly, truly, - thankful. In Christ name I give You Thanks.

• Thank you for Orec being Safe today. Father only you can give me this kind of day AMEN......

• Thank the Father for all the gifs you have prepared for me to walk in with the courage and Strength that also comes from you. All perfect gifts come from your Father Thanks.

• Thank you for a beautiful night that I am sure it's on its way. Full moon and Peace. Father right on!!! ....

• Thank you father for making my life fun, fun and funny!

Write Something that you're thankful for:

DAY TWENTY - FOUR

- Thank You Father God for a lock on gate.

- Thank you Father for the last adjustment on leg. It seems to be the best adjustment- so far

- Thank you Father for never leaving me.

- Thank you for the new wheel chair

- Thank you Father for such a nice day.

- Thank you Father for loving me.

- Father thank you for giving me money to share with others.

- Father thank you for giving me the wisdom to share. (How toy).

- Thank you Father I trust you that you won't let me be cheated by the Torres family.

Write Something that you're thankful for:

DAY TWENTY - FIVE

- Thank you Father for protecting me from those who would stilly kills, or destroy me.

- Father thank you for giving me the Help I need when you believe I need it. Not when I think I need it.

- Thank Father for a nice day.

- Thank you Father for the will to do your will.

- Father thank you for the power get wealth

- Thank you Father for the fruit that a bounds to Love.

- Father Thank you for helping to guard my mouth.

Write Something that you're thankful for:

DAY TWENTY – SIX

- Thank you Father for giving me parents that left me a home.

- Thank you Father for the land you choose for me to start over.

- Thank you, Father, for making share I never with alone.

- Thank you Father for god teachers

- Thank you father for transportation.

- Thank you Father for your Favor that's came

- Thank you Father for your mercy toward me.

- Thank you Father for your strength in me

- Thank your Father for your Joy toward me (in me)

- Thank you Father for your peace in me

- (In Christ Jesus I am Grateful)

Write Something that you're thankful for:

    MICHAEL E ZITO I

DAY TWENTY - SEVEN

- Thank you Lord for teaching me
How to think about my prayer life.

- Thank you Father for a not give up attitude.

- Thank you Farther for giving me
the ability to see you 24/7

- Thank you Father for wealth.

- Thank You Father for wisdom

- Thank you Father for teaching
me the fear of the Lord.

- Thank you Holy Spirit for making
share I understand God's word
for me on a daily pass

- Thank you Father for T.U. Ministers

Write Something that you're thankful for:

....

....

....

....

....

....

....

....

....

....

................Write Something that you're thankful for:...........

....

DAY TWENTY - EIGHT

- I Love You Father. Thank you Father for keeping me in the STORMS

- Thank you Father for the Love that gives of its self

- Thank you for giving me people to help me walk through Life, for I know I am not to walk alone. Not All of the time anyway.

- Thank you Father for being my Land-LORD.

- Thank you Father for helping me be a good start

- Thanks please give me a Strong desire to do your will Father Help me to Love reading and writing. Thank you Father for giving me a desire to fellowship with you. Father thank for strengthen my resolve.

Write Something that you're thankful for:

DAY TWENTY - NINE

- Thank you Father for making my life a success.

- Thank you Father for giving us the power, the grace to renew our minds

- Thank you Father for giving us the - Mind of Christ.

- Thank you Father for healing our land.

- Thank you Father for Healing all our diseases

- Thank you Father for forgiving all our iniquity

- Thank your father for not holding our sins against us

- Thank you Father for making it rain when we need water

Write Something that you're thankful for:

DAY THIRTY

- Father Thank You for this moment.

- Father Thank You for the rain today.

- Father Thank You for communing with me,

- Father Thank You for the fellowship of the Hay Spirit.

- Father I give you thanks in Christ Jesus name.

- Father Thank you for all the wild animals around Here.

- Father Thank you for giving me strength to move around this day.

- Father Thank you for making Oreo we all.

- Father Thank you for healing LA DAVID.

Write Something that you're thankful for:

 MICHAEL E ZITO I

DAY THIRTY - ONE

- Father thank you for the snow.

- Father thank you for Wealth,

- Father thank you for daily bread.

- Father thank you for labors. (helpers)

- Father thank you for friends.

- Father thank you for wood to burn.

- Father thank you for keeping me from evil.

- Father thank you for given me strength

- Father thank you for making me a giver.

- Father thank you for the patience

- Father thank you for loving us

- Thank you for your encouragement

Write Something that you're thankful for:

     MICHAEL E ZITO I

DAY THIRTY - TWO

- Father Thank You for saving me.

- Father Thank you making
some good out of me

- Father Thank you for strengthen me

- Father Thank you for providing everything
that pertains to this life and Godliness

- Father Thank you that you have the answer

- Father Thank you for the
Revelation of your LOVE

- Father Thank you for being trust worthy

Write Something that you're thankful for:

DAY THIRTY - THREE

- Thank You Father for stopping
the bleeding (Psalm 107.20)

"20 He sent out his word and healed them, and delivered them from their destruction. 20 He sent out his word and healed them, snatching them from the door of death. 20 He spoke the word that healed you, that pulled you back from the brink of death."

- Thank you Father for saving me from death

- Thank you Father for making me
part of your family. (Psalm 105:41)

41 He opened the rock, and water gushed out; it flowed like a river in the desert. 42 For he remembered his holy promise given to his servant Abraham. 45 that they might keep his precepts and observe his laws. Praise the LORD.

- Thank You Father for you are good.

(Psalm 107:1)
"Give thanks to the LORD, for he is good!
His faithful love endures forever."

- Thank your Father for redeeming
  me from the hand of my enemy

(Psalm 107:2)
2 Let the redeemed of the Lord say so,
whom he hath redeemed from the hand
of the enemy; 3 And gathered them out
of the lands, from the east, and from the
west, from the north, and from the south.

- Thank you Father for gathering
  me together with others of yaks

(Psalm 107:3)
3 And gathered them out of the lands,
from the east, and from the west,
from the north, and from the south.
4 They wandered in the wilderness
in a solitary way; they found no city
to dwell in. 5 Hungry and thirsty,
their soul fainted in them.

- Thank you father for out of my distresses

- Thank you that you lead me and guide me

(Psalm 107:7)
7 He led them by a straight way till they reached a city to dwell in. 7 He led them straight to safety, to a city where they could live. 7 He put your feet on a wonderful road that took you straight to a good place to live.

- Thank you Father for all
  your wonderful works

(Psalm 107:8)
'Let them give thanks to the LORD for his unfailing love and his wonderful deeds for mankind"

Write Something that you're thankful for:

DAY THIRTY – FOUR

• Father God Thank You for the
Provision Promises by Joseph Prince

• Thank You Farther for delivering
them from their distress.

(Psalm 107:6)
**"Then they cried unto the LORD in their
trouble, and he delivered them out of
their distresses. 6 Then they cried to the
LORD in their trouble, and he delivered
them from their distress. 6 "LORD,
help!" they cried in their trouble, and
he rescued them from their distress."**

• Thank you LORD for your steadfast love

(Psalm 107:8)
**"Let them give thanks to the LORD
for his unfailing love and his
wonderful deeds for mankind."**

• Thank you Father for satisfying my soul

(Psalm 107:9)
**"For he satisfies the longing soul, and the
hungry soul he fills with good things"**

- Thank you Rather Erd for delivering
me from my God distress

(Psalm 107:13)
"Then they cried to the LORD
in their trouble, and he saved
them from their distress"

- Thank You Father for
bringing me out of death

(Psalm 107:14)
"He brought them out of
darkness, the utter darkness,
and broke away their chains"

- Thank your Father for saving me
when I have been at my wits end

(Psalm 107:27)
"They reeled and staggered like
drunkards; they were at their wits' end."

- 8 Thank you Father for stopping
the bad terms of life.

(Psalm 107 29)
"He made the storm be still, and the
waves of the sea were hushed."

- Thank you Father for bringing me
home safe from my trips to town

Write Something that you're thankful for:

DAY THIRTY – FIVE

- Thank you, Father, for forgetting my sins a lawlessness.

- Thank you Father for forgetting my bad deeds

- Thank you Father for forgetting my sins, inequities, and transgressions.

- Thank you Father for never ever using my past against me

- Father thank you for my reading glasses.

- Father that you for good Christian writers.

Write Something that you're thankful for:

DAY THIRTY - SIX

- Hallelujah! Thank you Father for giving me such a wonderful life and that life eternally

- Thank you Father for the Bible and Revelation to know you and the fellowship of your suffering

- Thank you Father for all your weather.

- Thank you Father for good clean running water.

- Thank you Father for all kinds of weather

- Thank you father for all the seasons of life.

- Thank you Father for sunshine.

- Thank you Father for the wind

- Thank you Father for the rain

Write Something that you're thankful for:

....

....

....

....

....

....

....

....

....

....

....

....

DAY THIRTY – SEVEN

- Father Thank You for always hearing my prayers; Father Thank You for always seeing me.

(Psalm -34:15)
"The eyes of the Lord are on the righteous, and his ears are attentive to their cry"

- Father Thank You for always seeing me.

- Father Thank you for Blessing me in your refuge

(Psalm -34:8)
"Taste and see that the Lord is good; blessed is the one who takes refuge in him."

- Father Thank for seeing that those who worship you, lack nothing

(Psalm -34:9)
"Fear the Lord, you his holy people, for those who fear him lack nothing."

- Father God Thank you for
delivering me from way fears.

(Psalm -34:4)
"I sought the LORD, and he answered
me; he delivered me from all my fears."

- Thank you father that you hear a poor
man's cry, and save him out of all his troubles

(Psalm -34:6)
"This poor man called, and the
LORD heard him; he saved him
out of all his troubles."

- Thank you, father, for always being with us

(Psalm -34:7)
"The angel of the LORD encamps
around those who fear him,
and he delivers them."

- Thank you Father for delivering
us from all afflictions

(Psalm -34:19)
"The righteous person may have
many troubles, but the LORD
delivers him from them all;"

Write Something that you're thankful for:

....

....

....

....

....

....

....

....

....

....

..........................Write Something that you're thankful for:..........

....

DAY THIRTY – EIGHT

- Father Thank you for the heart's desire (HOLY Desire) you have planted in my Heart

(PSALM-37:4)
"Delight yourself in the Lord, and he will give you the desires of your heart."

- THANK Father for saving me out of all my troubles

(Psalms 34:6)
"6 This poor man cried, and the LORD heard him, and saved him out of all his troubles. 6 This poor man cried, and the LORD heard him and saved him out of all his troubles. 6 In my desperation I prayed, and the LORD listened; he saved me from all my troubles."

- Thank you Father for hearing me when I pray. (Even without speaking a word.)

(PSALM-37:14)
**"The wicked draw the sword and bend the
bow to bring down the poor and needy,
to slay those whose ways are upright.
15 But their swords will pierce their own
hearts, and their bows will be broken."**

- Thank you lead for being my salvation

(PSALM-35:3)
**"Draw out also the spear, and stop the
way against them that persecute me:
Say unto my soul, I am thy salvation."**

Write Something that you're thankful for:

....

....

....

....

....

....

....

....

....

....

....

....

DAY THIRTY – NINE

PSALM 91
"Bible Gateway Psalm 91: NIV. He who dwells in the shelter of the Most High will rest in the shadow of the Almighty. I will say of the LORD, "He is my refuge and my fortress, my God, in whom I trust." Surely he will save you from the fowler's snare and from the deadly pestilence."

- Thank You Father for being my protector.

  - Thank you Father for delivering me from the snare of trouble.

  - Thank you Father for delivering me from my daily pestilence.

    - Thank you for deliver me from fear of pestilence.

  - Thank You father that he plague will come near my Home.

  - Thank you Father for saving me Angels to guard me in all my ways.

- Father thank you for a long and healthy life.

  - Father thank you from keeping me in troubles that I could handle.

Write Something that you're thankful for:

DAY FORTY - ONE

- Thank you LORD for delivering me from all my fears.

- Thank you Father for making my face radiant and unashamed.

- Thank Father for saving me out of my troubles.

(PSALM 34:4-6)
"4 I sought the LORD, and he answered me; he delivered me from all my fears. 5 Those who look to him are radiant; their faces are never covered with shame. 6 This poor man called, and the LORD heard him; he saved him out of all his troubles."

- Thank you LORD for contending with these who fight against me.

(PSALM 31:1)
"1 In you, LORD, I have taken refuge; let me never be put to shame; deliver me in your righteousness."

- Thank you LORD for delivering the poor from him who is too strong for him.

PSALM 35:10
"10 My whole being will exclaim, "Who is like you, LORD? You rescue the poor from those too strong for them, the poor and needy from those who rob them."

- Thank you for protecting my assets.

(MALACHI 3:11)
"And I will rebuke the devourer for your sakes, and he shall not destroy the fruits of your ground; neither shall your vine cast her fruit before the time in the field, Faith the LORD of hosts."

Write Something that you're thankful for:

DAY FORTY - ONE

Father thank you for always
sending someone to help me.

Write Something that you're thankful for:

DAY FORTY – TWO

- Thank you Father that there is now no more condemnation because I am in Christ Jesus

- Father thank you that I am the righteousness of God in Christ Jesus.

- Thank you Father for your grace today that helps me overcome todays Challenge

Write Something that you're thankful for:

DAY FORTY - THREE

- Father thank you for redeeming
me through Jesus blood.

(Ephesians 1:7)
**"⁷ In him we have redemption
through his blood, the forgiveness
of sins, in accordance with the
riches of God's grace"**

- Father thank you for water,
good clean water.

- Father thank you for running water.

- Father thank you for Hot water

- Father thank you for my bath tub-that- hold
winter. When I play the whole
HA HA!

- Father thank you for the sunshine today.

- Father, thank you for grass the
kind you walk on HA! HA!

Write Something that you're thankful for:

DAY FORTY - FOUR

- Thank you Father for giving me freedom.

- Thank you Father for wisdom

- Thank you Father for ever increasing faith.

- Thank you Father for grace and more grace

- Thank you for my phone

- Thank you, Father for Wayne McMillan,

- Thank you Father for the friends you given Wayne M

- Thank you Father for the friends you have given me.

- Thank ye father for the Van.

- Thank you Father for the land

- Thank you Father for my motorcycle.

Write Something that you're thankful for:

DAY FORTY - FIVE

- Thank You Father for the new convent

- Thank You Father for taking such
  care of me, us, and them. Amen

- Thank You Father for giving me the
  ability to fare care of the animals

- Father thank you for the weeds
  … I pray the woods would be made
  well. The forest looks like its dying.
  Make It Love again please.

- Thank You Father for the pond
  and the fish and frogs in it. May they
  prosper and be in good heath

- Thank you Father for more and
  more revelation of the truth.

Write Something that you're thankful for:

DAY FORTY – SIX

1 Thessalonians 5:23
"23 May God himself, the God of peace, sanctify you through and through. May your whole spirit, soul and body be kept blameless at the coming of our Lord Jesus Christ."

- Thank You Father That you will keep me blameless at the coming of our Lord Jesus Christ.

- Thank You that the God of peace himself will sanctify me and completely and may my whole spirit and soul and body be kept.

- Father thank you for giving me so many chances to do what it is you will have me do every day

- Father thank you for being faithful

• Father thank you for giving me a delightful inheritance Further thank you for given me counsel.

"6 The boundary lines have fallen for me in pleasant places; surely I have a delightful inheritance.7 I will praise the Lᴏʀᴅ, who counsels me; even at night my heart instructs me."

Write Something that you're thankful for:

DAY FORTY - SEVEN

- Father Thank you that Jesus
  saves. to the utmost.

(Hebrews 7:25):
"therefore he is able to save
completely those who come to God
through him, because he always
lives to intercede for them."

- Thank you Father that we have peace
  with you through our Lord Jesus CHRST

(Romans 5:1)
"Therefore, since we have been justified
through faith, we have peace with God
through our Lord Jesus Christ."

- Thank you Father that through Christ
  whom also we have access by faith
  into this grace in which we stand, and
  rejoice in hope of the glory of God.

- Thank to Father of our Lord Jesus Christ, who has blessed us with every spiritual blessing in the heavenly places in Christ

(Ephesians 1:3)
"³ Praise be to the God and Father of our Lord Jesus Christ, who has blessed us in the heavenly realms with every spiritual blessing in Christ."

- Thank you Father that by Jesus Christ We have redemption through His block

(Ephesians 1:7)
"⁷ In him we have redemption through his blood, the forgiveness of sins, in accordance with the riches of God's grace"

- Thank you Father that you have made us your beloved ones called to saints

(Roman 1:7)
"⁷ To all in Rome who are loved by God and called to be his holy people: Grace and peace to you from God our Father and from the Lord Jesus Christ."

Write Something that you're thankful for:

DAY FORTY - EIGHT

- Thank father that Christ that I am your servant proclaiming the way of salvation.

**(Acts 16:17 in Other Translations)
"17 The same followed Paul and us, and cried, saying, these men are the servants of the most high God, which shew unto us the way of salvation."**

- Thank you Father for we are buried with Jesus through baptism into death, that just as Christ was raised from the dead by the glory of the Father, even so we also should walk in newness of life

**(Romans 6:4)
"4 We were therefore buried with him through baptism into death in order that, just as Christ was raised from the dead through the glory of the Father, we too may live a new life."**

- Thank you Father for telling me that as many of us as were baptized into Christ-Jesus were baptized in to His death

(Roman 6:3)
**"³ Or don't you know that all of us
who were baptized into Christ Jesus
were baptized into his death?"**
- Father Thank you for making me
the temple of the Holy Spirit.

(1 Corinthians 6:19)
**"¹⁹ Do you not know that your bodies
are temples of the Holy Spirit, who
is in you, whom you have received
from God? You are not your own;"**

- Father thank for teaching me to see that
no one is justified by the law in the sight of
God is evident, for the just shall live by faith.

(Galatians 3:11)
**"11 Clearly no one who relies on the
law is justified before God, because
"the righteous will live by faith."**

- Father thank you that when I ask you for
your wisdom you freely give her to me

(James 1:5)
**"⁵ If any of you lacks wisdom,
you should ask God, who gives
generously to all without finding
fault, and it will be given to you."**

Write Something that you're thankful for:

DAY FORTY - NINE

- Father Thank you for making us sons of God through faith in Christ Jesus

- Father Thank you that it doesn't matter if we are Jews are Greed's or slaves or are free. It doesn't even matter whether we are male or female we are all one in Chest Jesus and 'n Christ's we are Abraham's seed and heirs according to the promise.

(Galatians 3:26-29)
"**26 So in Christ Jesus you are all children of God through faith, 27 for all of you who were baptized into Christ have clothed yourselves with Christ. 28 There is neither Jew nor Gentile, neither slave nor free, nor is there male and female, for you are all one in Christ Jesus. 29 If you belong to Christ, then you are Abraham's seed, and heirs according to the promise."**

- Then You Father that for making Christ Jesus our High Priest

(Hebrews 3:1)
"Therefore, holy brothers and sisters, who share in the heavenly calling, fix your thoughts on Jesus, whom we acknowledge as our apostle and high priest."

• I thank you my God concerning you for the grace of God which was given to you by Christ Jesus, that were enriched in everything by Him in all utterance and all knowledge even as the testimony of Christ was confirmed in you, so that you come short in no grift, eagerly waiting for the revelation of a Lord Jesus Christ.

1 Corinthians 1:4-7
"4 I always thank my God for you because of his grace given you in Christ Jesus. 5 For in him you have been enriched in every way—with all kinds of speech and with all knowledge— 6 God thus confirming our testimony about Christ among you. 7 Therefore you do not lack any spiritual gift as you eagerly wait for our Lord Jesus Christ to be revealed."

Write Something that you're thankful for:

DAY FIFTY

Thank you, Jesus, for coming to earth and going through a beat down. Plus, thank you for going to the cross and shedding your blood for the forgiveness of my sins. Thank you for dying and going to hell. So that I will not go there. Thank you for rising from the dead. And becoming the first born of many brethren. Because your rose from the dead, I to will rise from the dead.

Thank you that my faith in what you have done I have already died, buried, and rose again to sit at the right hand of God. As you are in Heaven so am I on earth.

Write Something that you're thankful for:

DAY FIFTY - ONE

LORD, I come to you with a grateful heart. I rejoice in knowing that you Love me and mine.

Thank you for drawing me to spend time with you. Almighty God I am very grateful for your anointing in my Life.

Write Something that you're thankful for:

DAY FIFTY – TWO

**Father HOLY Father Thank you for in my
Your Kingdom come and for you will being
done on earth in my life as it is in Heaven.**

**Thank u for getting me back on
the path that you want me on.**

**There is nothing better than being
in the center of your will. GOD Bless
You LORD! Thank you for getting
me caught up on my bills.**

**Thank you, Father, for how you took care
of my Pate bills. Bless your Holy names.
Thank you for patience with me. Merciful
Father, I give you glory. Thank You Father
setting me up with Perris Tappice**

She will be a good I.H.S. worker for me.

Write Something that you're thankful for:

DAY FIFTY - THREE

Thank you, Father, for helping me take care of the animals in my life.

Thank you, Father, for eyes to see your word, written and the word that "has come to pass in my life, and in the life of though I have prayed for.

Thank you, Father, for protecting me from my enemies. Father Thank you for the friends that you have given me.

Father thank you for good food, and good clothes. Father thank you for a home with cunning water and electricity, Praise your HOLY NAMES,

Father God thank you for giving me Medical Insurance. AMEN

Father GOD Thank you for giving the ability to read. Thank you to giving me understanding and wisdom. AMEN…

Write Something that you're thankful for:

DAY FIFTY - FOUR

Father thank you for healing me and making me whole. From the top of my head to the souls of my feet: Thank you LORD for a nice day to drive and pick up the supplies that we need around here.

Write Something that you're thankful for:

DAY FIFTY - FIVE

Oh, give thanks to the LORD!
Call upon His name.
Make know his deeds among the people.
Sing to Him, sing Psalms to him.
Talk of all His wondrous works.
Glory in His holy name.
Let the hearts of those rejoice who.
Seek the LORD.
Seek the LORD and His strength.
Seek His face evermore!

(PSALM 105:1-4)
"1 Give praise to the LORD,
proclaim his name;
make known among the nations
what he has done.
2 Sing to him, sing praise to him;
tell of all his wonderful acts.
3 Glory in his holy name;
let the hearts of those who
seek the LORD rejoice.
4 Look to the LORD and his strength;
seek his face always."

Write Something that you're thankful for:

DAY FIFTY – SIX

Thank you, Father, for the new coffee
pot. Your timing is always right on time.
Bless you my father, have fun today as
you move among your people. I love you,
Father. Thank you, Father, for you alone
on we me lay down in peace. For you
LORD, only make me dwell in safety. Thank
you, Father, for keeping me safe from the
enemies of my soul. Thank you, Father,
for the desire to spend time seeking your
presence in my life. I love you. Father God.

Write Something that you're thankful for:

DAY FIFTY – SEVEN

Enter his gates with thanksgiving, and into his courts with praise; be thankful unto him and bless His name. For the LORD is good; his mercy is everlasting; and his truth endures to all generations.

(Psalm 100: 4-5)
"Enter his gates with thanksgiving and his courts with praise; give thanks to him and praise his name. 5 For the LORD is good and his love endures forever; his faithfulness continues through all generations."

Thank You Father for saving me for your purposes; may your will be done not mine. LORD God.

Write Something that you're thankful for:

DAY FIFTY – EIGHT

Thank you, Father, and the Lord Jesus
Christ for saving me from all sins.

So that I could walk without Sin
and live unto righteousness.

Thank Jesus for healing all my wounds
and diseases. Thank you, Holy Spirit,
for making me whole again.

Write Something that you're thankful for:

DAY FIFTY - NINE

"Thank you EL SHADDAI The almighty one that I need. You make sure I get everything I need and more. I Love You Father thank you for the firewood and blessed thoughts that are bringing the word to me and then machines."

Write Something that you're thankful for:

 MICHAEL E ZITO I

DAY SIXTY

**Thank You my great Father for giving
me the wisdom and the discernment
I need to make it through this life
without being a pad for my enemies.**

**Thank You for teaching me that there is a
VASS difference between the mind of the
Soul and the mind of the Spirit Help me
to always know the difference, before I
respond on re-asked in a righteous way.
Thank you, Father, for all the opportunities
you give me to minister Love to people.
MAY I always do a good Job of Loving
with each opportunity You give me.**

Write Something that you're thankful for:

DAY SIXTY - ONE

Thank You, Father, for allowing us to
vote for those ever us in this country.

Thank you even more for making
us rule with you eternally.

Thank you! Father for anointing my
head with oil my cut runs over.

Thank you for the goodness and mercy
that followed me all my life. mercy
Thank you for a nice, healthy day.

Thank you for the nice, healthy day.
Thank you for the joy of the Lord that
makes me strong in you AMEN.

Write Something that you're thankful for:

DAY SIXTY – TWO

Father thank you for keeping me
safe through. all my days. Safe
from physical harm today.

When I got in and out of the tub.

It is a danger time for me. Thank Father
God for abundance of clean water.
Thank you, Father, for giving me the
money to help other people have clean
water to drink and wash up with.

I hope to do a lot more for thought
without clean water in the future.

Thank you, Father, for the electricity.
If I didn't have electricity here, I
would not be able to pump the
water I heed up this mountain.

Write Something that you're thankful for:

DAY SIXTY – THREE

**Thank you, Father, for helping me
to Gridley CA and get my meds, and
return safely, to study your word.**

**Father it is so important that I remember
your words. Thank you for teaching me
to focus on what you have me to learn.**

**I love you Father, son and Holy
Spirit, I love you all to Angel's.**

Write Something that you're thankful for:

DAY SIXTY – FOUR

**Thank You Almighty Father for
your goodness that has led me
to repent from my sins.**

**Thank you for Helping me see that I
was wrong in the way I was spending
the time you give me to spend.**

**Spending time your way brings
me happiness and Joy. Think
Enter You Father, In Jesus name
I give you, my Thanks.**

Write Something that you're thankful for:

DAY SIXTY - FIVE

Thank you, Father, for giving me boldness
to peak to people about the word of God.
Help me to always use your wisdom when
talking to others about not only the word
of God but speaking in genome. Thank
you, Father, for giving me strength to live
every day with you. In Jesus name Amen

Write Something that you're thankful for:

DAY SIXTY – SIX

Thank you, Father, for your patience
with me. I give you thanks my Lord for
never leaving me nor for seeking me.

Oh! Give thanks to the LORD,
for he is good. for his steadfast
love endures forever!

Write Something that you're thankful for:

DAY SIXTY – SEVEN

**You are my God Father, and I will give
thanks to you; you are my God, I will extol
you. Thank You Father for you righteous
promise. Thank you, Father, for your love.**

**Thank you, Father for your Holy Bible,
In Jesus Christ. Amen. Hallelujah!**

Write Something that you're thankful for:

DAY SIXTY – EIGHT

Father, thank you for meeting all our
needs according to your wealth.

Father thank you for raising us nearer
and nearer to thee. Thank you that we can
know you more and more if we want to.

I want to know you better and
better. In Jesus name …

Father thank you for never ever leaving
us alone to face this world by ourselves.

Write Something that you're thankful for:

DAY SIXTY – NINE

Father God Thank you for sending.
Jesus to make away for us to be
together again as Father and son.

Thank you, Jesus, for being obedient to
the Father so we can be a family again.

Thank you, Father, for giving me
Mequel and his Family and. friends.
To Help me through this life.

Father Save them and make them
all your sons and my brothers.

Help us to understand one
another and love one another.
In Jesus name. I pray you.

Write Something that you're thankful for:

DAY SEVENTY

Thank you Father God for a good running
van. Thank you Father for keeping me
safe as I have driven it.
Thank you Father for keeping others
safe as they drive it. Thank you
God for giving me the money when
I need it; so that I can have the
maintenance kept up on it.
In Christ name: Amen.

Write Something that you're thankful for:

DAY SEVENTY – ONE

Father thank you for taking me
Wife Debbie into your loving
presence. Father thank you for
friends that are helping me during
this season of grieving me
wife's passing. In Jesus name I
praise you for your loving care of
your Children. Father thank you that
Your children do not grieve like those.
who have no hope in you, But?
those who do know and love you LORD.

Write Something that you're thankful for:

DAY SEVENTY – TWO

Father Thank you for Blessing
the person who walks not in the
counsel of the wicked, nor stands.
in the way of sinners, nor sits.
in the set of scoffers; but
his delight is in the law of the
LORD, and on his law the person
meditates day and night. In Jesus
name. Amen

(Psalm 1:1-2).
**"1 Blessed is the one who does
not walk in step with the wicked or
stand in the way that sinners take or
sit in the company of mockers,
2 but whose delight is in the law
of the LORD, and who meditates
on his law day and night."**

Write Something that you're thankful for:

DAY SEVENTY - THREE

Thank You Father God for telling
us to your Son (Jesus Christ)
lest you be angry, and we perish.
in the way, for his wrath is quickly
handled. Blessed on all who take
refuge in him.

(Psalm 2:12)
**"12 Kiss his son, or he will be angry
and your way will lead to your destruction,
for his wrath can flare up in a moment.
Blessed are all who take refuge in him."**

Write Something that you're thankful for:

DAY SEVENTY - FOUR

Thank You O LORD for you bless
the Righteous, O LORD you cover.
him with art favor as with a shield.

(PSALM 5:12)
"12 Surely, Lᴏʀᴅ, you bless the righteous;
you surround them with your
favor as with a shield."

Write Something that you're thankful for:

DAY SEVENTY - FIVE

Father thank you that you gave me
an assignment. Thank you that when
we seek first the kingdom of
God and his righteous. That you
will give to anyone that seeks you.
Something to do that glorifies.
you.

Write Something that you're thankful for:

DAY SEVENTY – SIX

LORD God on you do I wait all
the day. Help me always to be
thankful. Thank you Father that in
Christ Jesus you forgive all my us
iniquity, and heal all my diseases,
you redeem my life from the pit,
You crown me with steadfast love
and mercy, you satisfy me with good.
so that my youth is renewed like the
eagles.

(Psalm 103:1-5)
"1 Praise the LORD, my soul;
all my inmost being, praise his holy name.
2 Praise the LORD, my soul,
and forget not all his benefits—
3 who forgives all your sins
and heals all your diseases,
4 who redeems your life from the pit
and crowns you with love and compassion,
5 who satisfies your desires with good things
so that your youth is renewed
like the eagle's."

Write Something that you're thankful for:

DAY SEVENTY – SEVEN

Thank Father God for sol loving the
World, that you gave your only Son,
that whoever believes in him should
not perish but have eternal life.
For God did not send his Son
Into the world to condemn the world
But in order that the world might
Be saved through him. Thank you Jesus
Christ for cheering the Father.

(Read John 3:16)
"16 For God so loved the world that
he gave his one and only Son, that
whoever believes in him shall not
perish but have eternal life."

Write Something that you're thankful for:

DAY SEVENTY – EIGHT

Oh give thanks to the LORD;
call upon his name, make known.
his deeds among the peoples!
Sing to him, sing praises to him,
tell of all his wondrous weeks!
Glory in his holy name; let the
hearts of those who seek the LORD.
rejoice! Seek the LORD and his
Strength seek his presence
Continually!

(READ: PSALM 105.)
"32 He turned their rain into hail,
with lightning throughout their land;
33 he struck down their vines and fig trees
and shattered the trees of their country.
34 He spoke, and the locusts came,
grasshoppers without number;
35 they ate up every green
thing in their land,
ate up the produce of their soil.
36 Then he struck down all the
firstborn in their land,
the first fruits of all their manhood.

37 He brought out Israel, laden
with silver and gold,
and from among their tribe's
no one faltered.
38 Egypt was glad when they left,
because dread of Israel
had fallen on them.
39 He spread out a cloud as a covering,
and a fire to give light at night.
40 They asked, and he brought them quail;
he fed them well with the bread of heaven.
41 He opened the rock, and
water gushed out;
it flowed like a river in the desert.
42 For he remembered his holy promise
given to his servant Abraham.
43 He brought out his
people with rejoicing,
his chosen ones with shouts of joy;
44 he gave them the lands of the nations,
and they fell heir to what
others had toiled for—
45 that they might keep his precepts
and observe his laws.
Praise the LORD"

Write Something that you're thankful for:

DAY SEVENTY - NINE

At last supper before the Lord
went to suffer for mankind.
He took bread, gave thanks and
broke it, and gave it to them, saying.
"This is my body which is given for you,
do this in remembrance of ME,
Likewise, He also took the cup after
supper, saying, this cup is the new
**covenant in My blood, which
is shed for you"**

READ: (Luke 22:19-20)
**"19 And he took bread, gave thanks
and broke it, and gave it to them,
saying, "This is my body given for
you; do this in remembrance of me."
20 In the same way, after the supper
he took the cup, saying, "This cup
is the new covenant in my blood,
which is poured out for you"**

Thank You Lord Jesus for all
You have done for US in your Suffering

Write Something that you're thankful for:

DAY EIGHTY

Give thanks in all circumstances,
for this is the will of God in
Christ Jesus for you. Thank you
Father in these hard times; for.
without you Father they would be.
many whores.

(Read I Thessalonians.5 - 18)
"18 give thanks in all circumstances; for
this is God's will for you in Christ Jesus."

Write Something that you're thankful for:

DAY EIGHTY- ONE

Oh give thanks to the LORD, He
Is good; for his steadfast love endures
forever!

READ: (Psalm 118:1-21)
"1 Give thanks to the LORD, for he is good;
his love endures forever.
2 Let Israel say:
"His love endures forever."
3 Let the house of Aaron say:
"His love endures forever."
4 Let those who fear the LORD say:
"His love endures forever."
5 When hard pressed, I cried to the LORD;
he brought me into a spacious place.
6 The LORD is with me; I will not be afraid.
What can mere mortals do to me?
7 The LORD is with me; he is my helper.
I look in triumph on my enemies.
8 It is better to take refuge in the LORD
than to trust in humans.
9 It is better to take refuge in the LORD
than to trust in princes.
10 All the nations surrounded me,

but in the name of the LORD
I cut them down.
11 They surrounded me on every side,
but in the name of the LORD
I cut them down.
12 They swarmed around me like bees,
but they were consumed as
quickly as burning thorns;
in the name of the LORD I cut them down.
13 I was pushed back and about to fall,
but the LORD helped me.
14 The LORD is my strength
and my defense;
he has become my salvation.
15 Shouts of joy and victory
resound in the tents of the righteous:
"The LORD's right hand has
done mighty things!
16 The LORD's right hand is lifted high;
the LORD's right hand has
done mighty things!"
17 I will not die but live,
and will proclaim what the LORD has done.
18 The LORD has chastened me severely,
but he has not given me over to death.
19 Open for me the gates of the righteous;
I will enter and give thanks to the LORD.
20 This is the gate of the LORD

**through which the righteous may enter.
21 I will give you thanks, for you answered
me; you have become my salvation.**

I thank you that you have answered
Me and have become my salvation

Write Something that you're thankful for:

DAY EIGHTY- TWO

Thank you Father for the Holy Spirit;
thank you have given us so that we
will be able to live the life of Grace
that. Jesus Christ dies to give us.
To enable us to do what we could
never do without Him. In Jesus name
Father I give You" my thanksgiving.

Write Something that you're thankful for:

DAY EIGHTY- THREE

Father thank you for Doctors and medicine. Father thank you for the Suffering of this present time is nothing worth comparing with the glory that is to be revealed to us.
In Jesus name.

(Read Romans 8:18)
"18 I consider that our present sufferings are not worth comparing with the glory that will be revealed in us."

Write Something that you're thankful for:

....

....

....

....

....

....

....

....

....

....

....

....

DAY EIGHTY- FOUR

Father thank you for the gifts
You give to your people including the
first gift you gave your Church in
the upper room the gift of the
Holy Spirit with the resentence of
Speaking in tongues. In Jesus name

(Read Acts 2:2-4)
**"2 Suddenly a sound like the blowing of a
violent wind came from heaven and filled
the whole house where they were sitting.
3 They saw what seemed to be tongues
of fire that separated and came to rest
on each of them. 4 All of them were filled
with the Holy Spirit and began to speak in
other tongues as the Spirit enabled them."**

Write Something that you're thankful for:

DAY EIGHTY- FIVE

Father thank you for the power.
to be your witnesses in all the
world. In Jesus name

(Read Acts 1:8)
"8 But you will receive power when the Holy
Spirit comes on you; and you will be my
witnesses in Jerusalem, and in all Judea and
Samaria, and to the ends of the earth.""

Write Something that you're thankful for:

DAY EIGHTY- SIX

Thank you Father that every seemly
bad in our life's death of loved ones
pain and things we just don't
understand. Is working for good
to through of us who love you.
and are called according to your purpose.

Read (Romans 8:28)
"28 And we know that in all things God works
for the good of those who love him, who
have been called according to his purpose."

Write Something that you're thankful for:

DAY EIGHTY- SEVEN

Father God Thank you for my Home
and for Electricity and Hot and cold
running water. Thank You Father for
a wood burning store and for the
paper and wood to burn. Thank You
Father for food and clothing.
Thank you Father for the strength
it takes to live we all each day.
In Jesus name Amen.

Write Something that you're thankful for:

DAY EIGHTY- EIGHT

Thank You LORD God for you hear
your people's cry for help. Thank you
Father for you rescues us from all
our troubles

**See (Psalm 34:17-18)
"17 The righteous cry out, and
the LORD hears them;
he delivers them from all their troubles.
18 The LORD is close to the brokenhearted
and saves those who are
crushed in spirit."**

Write Something that you're thankful for:

DAY EIGHTY- NINE

Thank you Father God! For many are
The afflictions of the Righteous
But the LORD delivers us out of
them all. In Jesus name

(See Psalm 34: 19-20)
"19 The righteous person may
have many troubles,
but the LORD delivers him from them all;
20 he protects all his bones,
not one of them will be broken."

Write Something that you're thankful for:

....

....

....

....

....

....

....

....

....

....

....

....

DAY NINETY

Thank you Father for blessing the
one's who consider the needs of
the poor. Thank you LORD for
sustaining them on their sick bed
in their illness you restore them to
full Health. As for me, I said, O
LORD, be gracious to me, heal me
for I have sinned against you.

(See. Psalm 11:1-4)
1 In the LORD I take refuge.
How then can you say to me:
"Flee like a bird to your mountain.
2 For look, the wicked bend their bows;
they set their arrows against the strings
to shoot from the shadows
at the upright in heart.
3 When the foundations
are being destroyed,
what can the righteous do?"
4 The LORD is in his holy temple;
the LORD is on his heavenly throne.
He observes everyone on earth;
his eyes examine them.

Write Something that you're thankful for:

DAY NINETY- ONE

Offer to God a sacrifice of
Thanksgiving, and perform your vows.
to The Highest, and call upon me in
the day of trouble; I will deliver you.
and you Shall glorify me.

READ (Psalm 50:14-15)
"14 "Sacrifice thank offerings to God,
fulfill your vows to the Most High,
15 and call on me in the day of trouble;
I will deliver you, and you will honor me."

Write Something that you're thankful for:

....

....

....

....

....

....

....

....

....

....

....

....

DAY NINETY- TWO

Praise the LORD! I will give thanks
to the LORD with my whole heart,
in the company of the upright, in the
congregation
I praise and give thanks
in the gathering of the Saints
To The LORD my Father I thank you
when I am alone; or in the presence.
of the world. In the doctor's office
or in the grocery store. Father
thank you. In Christ name Amen.

Write Something that you're thankful for:

DAY NINETY- THREE

Father I'm so thankful for you
seeking me, That I just want to
seek you right back! I get cc
big kick out of us seeking to
know each other. I know Father that
You know everything about me. However,
as I talk to you about you I find me
I Love you so very much! PAD.

Write Something that you're thankful for:

DAY NINETY- FOUR

Father my father you are so wonderful
time and mine that I am glad that you allow
me to share my thanks with everyone
that fends what you have allowed me to
right down. Thank you Father for talking.
to me and to all people Gail Haire for
the Spiritual ears we need to hear with.
In Jesus name I give you thanks.

Write Something that you're thankful for:

DAY NINETY- FIVE

**I will praise the name of God with a song;
I will magnify with Thanksgiving- Him**

**(Read Psalm 69:30)
"I will praise God's name in song and
glorify him with thanksgiving."**

Thank you Father for Helping me to sing well!
Space for Thanks People of
GOD... pace for your Thanks.
100 days. OF Thanksgiving

**I will praise the name of God with a song;
I will magnify with Thanksgiving- Him**

**(Read Psalm 69:30)
"I will praise God's name in song and
glorify him with thanksgiving."**

Thank you Father for Helping me to sing well!
Space for Thanks People of GOD...

Write Something that you're thankful for:

DAY NINETY- SIX

Father Thank you for your paints toward
us and your tiredness toward us. Thank
you, Father, for your m for your mercy
and grace toward Us. Father, thank
you for your relentless love for us!
In

Jesus Amen.

Write Something that you're thankful for:

DAY NINETY- SEVEN

Give thanks to the LORD call upon his name
make known his deeds among the people.
**O give thanks unto the LORD; for he
is good, for his mercy endures.**

Read (1 Chronicles 16.).
**"Give thanks to the LORD, for he is
good; his love endures forever. Cry out,
"Save us, O God our Savior; gather us
and deliver us from the nations, that
we may give thanks to your holy name,
that we may glory in your praise."**

Write Something that you're thankful for:

DAY NINETY- EIGHT

I'm Giving thanks always for all things unto God and the Father in the name of our Lord Jesus Christ; Submitting yourselves are to another in the fear of God.

Read (Ephesians 5:2–21)
2 and walk in the way of love, just as Christ loved us and gave himself up for us as a fragrant offering and sacrifice to God. 3 But among you there must not be even a hint of sexual immorality, or of any kind of impurity, or of greed, because these are improper for God's holy people. 4 Nor should there be obscenity, foolish talk or coarse joking, which are out of place, but rather thanksgiving. 5 For of this you can be sure: No immoral, impure or greedy person—such a person is an idolater—has any inheritance in the kingdom of Christ and of God. 6 Let no one deceive you with empty words, for because of such things God's wrath comes on those who are disobedient. 7 Therefore do not be partners with them.

8 For you were once darkness, but now you are light in the Lord. Live as children of light 9 (for the fruit of the light consists in all goodness, righteousness and truth) 10 and find out what pleases the Lord. 11 Have nothing to do with the fruitless deeds of darkness, but rather expose them. 12 It is shameful even to mention what the disobedient do in secret. 13 But everything exposed by the light becomes visible—and everything that is illuminated becomes a light. 14 This is why it is said:
"Wake up, sleeper,
rise from the dead,
and Christ will shine on you."
15 Be very careful, then, how you live—not as unwise but as wise, 16 making the most of every opportunity, because the days are evil.17 Therefore do not be foolish, but understand what the Lord's will is. 18 Do not get drunk on wine, which leads to debauchery. Instead, be filled with the Spirit, 19 speaking to one another with psalms, hymns, and songs from the Spirit. Sing and make music from your heart to the Lord, 20 always giving thanks to God the Father for everything, in the name of our Lord Jesus Christ.

DAY NINETY- NINE

Rejoice in the Lord always, and again
I say, Rejoice. Let your gentleness be
known unto all men. The Lord is at hand.
Be anxious for nothing; but in everything by
prayer and supplication with thanksgiving.
Let Your requests be made known unto God.
**And the Peace of God, which passes all
understanding, shall keep your hearts
and minds through Christ Jesus.**

(Philippians 4:4-9)
**[4]Rejoice in the Lord always. I will say
it again: Rejoice! [5]Let your gentleness
be evident to all. The Lord is near. [6]Do
not be anxious about anything, but in
everything, by prayer and petition, with
thanksgiving, present your requests
to God. [7]And the peace of God, which
transcends all understanding, will guard
your hearts and your minds in Christ
Jesus. [8]Finally, brothers, whatever is
true, whatever is noble, whatever is
right, whatever is pure, whatever is
lovely, whatever is admirable-if anything
is excellent or praiseworthy-think**

about such things. [9]Whatever you have learned or received or heard from me, or seen in me-put it into practice. And the God of peace will be with you.

Write Something that you're thankful for:

DAY ONE HUNDRED

I will give the LORD thanks due to his righteousness, and I will sing praise to the name of the LORD, the Highest. Thank You Father for you are the Highest God worthy of all our Thanksgiving.

Read (Psalm 7:17)
17 I will give thanks to the LORD
because of his righteousness;
I will sing the praises of the name
of the LORD Most High.

Write Something that you're thankful for:

CONCLUSION

Put on then, as God's chosen ones, holy and beloved, compassionate hearts, kindness, humility, meekness and patience, bearing with one another and, if one has a complaint against another, forgiving each other, as the Lord has forgiven you so you also must forgive. And let the peace of Christ rule in your hearts, to which indeed you were called in one body. And be thankful. Let the word of Christ dwell in you richly, Teaching and admonishing one another in all Wisdom, singing psalms and hymns and Spiritual Songs, with thankfulness in your hearts to God. And whatever you do, in word or deed, do everything in the name of the Lord Jesus, giving thanks to God the Father through Him.

(Read. Col.3:1-17)

Space for your Conclusion:

DEDICATION

**Special Thank you to ReadersMagnet
for being patient with me with
Publishing this book.**

**Thank you for my Project
Manager Kiarabelle.**

**And Also thank you Rizie Ejercito for
helping me with my manuscript.**

ABOUT THE AUTHOR

Michael Zito I have a friend named Ernie Griggs since mid-80" s and they both lived a bike lifestyle in 1992. He gave his friend a first Bible and was lead his friend to believe and serve God. Michael Zito I has a strong belief in God and his love for walking in Christ.

Your Brother in Christ
Ernie Griggs.

www.ingramcontent.com/pod-product-compliance
Lightning Source LLC
Chambersburg PA
CBHW060913140726
47996CB00001B/229